LILY GLADSTONE

Embracing Heritage, Shaping Hollywood –
A Journey of Talent, Identity, and
Trailblazing in Cinema

BY

BILLY NORA

Lily Gladstone

ACKNOWLEDGMENTS

I would like to express my deepest gratitude to everyone who contributed to the creation of this biography.

First and foremost, I extend my heartfelt thanks to Lily Gladstone for her remarkable journey and for allowing her story to be told. Your generosity, authenticity, and dedication to your craft are truly inspiring.

I owe a debt of gratitude to my family and friends for their unwavering encouragement, understanding, and patience during the countless hours spent researching and writing.

I am indebted to the readers and fans of Lily Gladstone whose passion for storytelling and appreciation for indigenous representation continue to inspire and motivate me.

Lastly, I would like to acknowledge the ancestors, elders, and indigenous communities whose resilience, wisdom, and cultural heritage continue to enrich our world.

Thank you all for being part of this journey.

Warm regards,

Billy Nora

TABLE OF CONTENT

CHAPTER 1

Roots Of Resilience

In the vast expanse of the American West, amidst the rugged beauty of the Blackfeet Reservation in northwestern Montana, Lily Gladstone's journey begins. Here, beneath the expansive skies and rolling plains, she inherits a legacy steeped in tradition, culture, and resilience.

The Blackfeet Legacy:

The Blackfeet Nation, with its rich tapestry of history and tradition, serves as the backdrop for Gladstone's early years. Born into a community deeply connected to the land and its teachings, she learned the importance of resilience, strength, and cultural pride from an early age. Raised by parents who instilled in her a deep reverence for her heritage, Gladstone's childhood is imbued with the rituals, stories, and values of her ancestors.

A Childhood on the Reservation:

For Gladstone, the reservation is more than just a place—it is a home, a sanctuary, and a source of identity. Here, amidst the close-knit community of family and friends, she experiences the warmth of communal living and the bonds of mutual reliance. From attending tribal ceremonies to listening to elders share stories of the past, she finds solace and belonging in the traditions of her people.

Transition to Suburbia:

At the age of eleven, Gladstone's world is upended as her family makes the difficult decision to leave the reservation in search of better economic opportunities. Transitioning from the vast expanse of the reservation to the confines of suburban life proves to be a daunting challenge for the young Gladstone. Suddenly thrust into a world of unfamiliar customs, cultures, and expectations, she grapples with feelings of displacement, isolation, and cultural disconnect.

Navigating Two Worlds:

As Gladstone adapts to life in the suburbs, she finds herself straddling two worlds—the familiar rhythms of reservation life and the alienating landscape of suburban America. While she embraces the opportunities afforded by her new surroundings, she yearns for the sense of community and belonging she left behind on the reservation. Despite the challenges of navigating cultural identity in a predominantly non-indigenous environment, Gladstone remains steadfast in her commitment to honoring her heritage and preserving her cultural identity.

The Influence of Family:

Throughout her formative years, Gladstone finds strength and support in the unwavering love and guidance of her family. Raised by parents who instilled in her a deep sense of pride, resilience, and cultural reverence, she learned the importance of staying true to herself and her heritage in the face of adversity. With their encouragement, she embraces her passion for storytelling and performance, setting her on a path toward self-discovery and fulfillment.

In the crucible of her early years on the Blackfeet Reservation and the transition to suburban life, Lily Gladstone's journey is forged. Rooted firmly in the customs of her ancestors and guided by the love and support of her family, she navigates the complexities of cultural identity with grace, resilience, and determination. As she embarks on the next chapter of her journey, she carries with her the lessons learned and the values instilled in her by her indigenous heritage—a legacy of resilience, strength, and cultural pride that will shape her path for years to come.

CHAPTER 2:

Nurturing The Flame Within

As Lily Gladstone navigates the intricate landscape of cultural identity and personal growth, she finds herself drawn to the transformative power of storytelling and performance. In this chapter, we delve into her journey of self-discovery, creative exploration, and the pursuit of her passion for acting.

Discovering the Stage:

From an early age, Gladstone is captivated by the magic of the stage—the thrill of inhabiting different worlds, embodying diverse characters, and connecting with audiences through the art of storytelling. Inspired by the rich oral traditions of her indigenous heritage, she finds solace and inspiration in the transformative power of performance.

Theatrical Beginnings:

Gladstone's journey into the world of acting begins with tentative steps on the local stage. From school productions to community theater, she hones her craft and discovers the joy of embodying characters, exploring emotions, and sharing stories with audiences. With each performance, she gains confidence, skill, and a deeper appreciation for the transformative power of the stage.

Nurturing Creativity:

As Gladstone's passion for acting blossoms, she seeks out opportunities to nurture her creativity and expand her artistic horizons. From acting classes to workshops, she immerses herself in the study of dramatic arts, soaking up knowledge, techniques, and insights from seasoned professionals and fellow performers. With each new experience, she grows as an artist, refining her skills and honing her craft.

Embracing Diversity:

In her journey as an actor, Gladstone embraces the diversity of human experience, seeking out roles that challenge her to inhabit different perspectives, cultures, and identities. From Shakespearean classics to contemporary dramas, she embraces the opportunity to explore the complexities of the human condition, shedding light on untold stories and amplifying marginalized voices through her performances.

The Power of Representation:

For Gladstone, acting is more than just a profession—it is a platform for advocacy, empowerment, and social change. As a proud Indigenous woman, she recognizes the importance of representation in the entertainment industry and strives to amplify the voices and stories of underrepresented communities. Through her work, she seeks to challenge stereotypes, dismantle barriers, and create space for diverse narratives to thrive.

Cultural Reverence:

Rooted in the customs of her indigenous heritage, Gladstone approaches acting with a deep sense of cultural reverence and responsibility. Drawing inspiration from the stories, teachings, and rituals of her ancestors, she infuses her performances with authenticity, integrity, and respect for indigenous wisdom and traditions. With each role, she honors the legacy of her ancestors and celebrates the resilience, strength, and cultural pride of indigenous peoples.

At this stage, Lily Gladstone's passion for acting is ignited, fueled by a deep-seated desire to connect, inspire, and transform. With each performance, she embarks on a journey of self-discovery, creative exploration, and cultural celebration, channeling the transformative power of storytelling to illuminate the human experience and amplify marginalized voices. As she continues to navigate the complexities of the entertainment industry, she remains steadfast in her commitment to authenticity, representation, and the pursuit of artistic excellence.

CHAPTER 3:

Breaking Barriers And Shaping Narratives

In this chapter, we delve into Lily Gladstone's journey as she confronts industry norms, challenges stereotypes, and reshapes narratives to reflect the rich diversity of human experience.

Challenging Stereotypes:

As Gladstone's career gains momentum, she confronts the pervasive stereotypes and narrowcasting practices that have long marginalized indigenous actors in the entertainment industry. Refusing to be confined by outdated tropes and limited representations, she boldly asserts her agency, challenging directors, producers, and casting agents to recognize the depth, complexity, and diversity of indigenous narratives.

Navigating Hollywood:

In the hallowed halls of Hollywood, Gladstone navigates the complex terrain of auditions, callbacks, and casting calls with resilience and determination. Despite facing systemic barriers and entrenched biases, she refuses to compromise her authenticity or sacrifice her cultural integrity for the sake of conformity. With each audition, she brings her unique perspective, lived experiences, and artistic vision to the table, carving out a space for herself in an industry that often overlooks indigenous talent.

Forging Partnerships:

As Gladstone's star continues to rise, she forges meaningful partnerships with directors, writers, and fellow actors who share her commitment to authenticity, representation, and social justice. Collaborating with like-minded creatives, she co-creates stories that challenge stereotypes, amplify marginalized voices, and reshape the cultural landscape of mainstream media. Together, they strive to dismantle barriers, broaden perspectives, and foster greater empathy and understanding across diverse communities.

Empowering Communities:

Beyond the glitz and glamour of the red carpet, Gladstone remains deeply rooted in her indigenous community, using her platform and visibility to empower, uplift, and inspire the next generation of indigenous talent. Through mentorship programs, outreach initiatives, and advocacy efforts, she works tirelessly to create pathways for aspiring actors, storytellers, and filmmakers to access opportunities, resources, and support networks within the entertainment industry. By nurturing talent, amplifying voices, and fostering solidarity, she catalyzes a cultural renaissance that celebrates indigenous resilience, creativity, and cultural pride.

Redefining Success:

In a culture obsessed with fame, fortune, and accolades, Gladstone redefines success on her own terms, prioritizing authenticity, integrity, and impact over fame and fortune. For her, the true measure of success lies not in box office receipts or awards ceremonies, but in the ability to create meaningful, transformative art that resonates with audiences, sparks conversations, and fosters positive social change. With each role, she seeks to challenge, inspire, and uplift, leaving a lasting legacy that transcends the fleeting glamour of the silver screen.

As Lily Gladstone continues to break barriers, shape narratives, and redefine success in the entertainment industry, she remains a beacon of hope, resilience, and possibility for indigenous talent around the world. With courage, conviction, and unwavering commitment, she paves the way for a more inclusive, equitable, and diverse media landscape, where every voice is heard, every story is valued, and every dream is within reach. In her journey, she embodies the power of storytelling to transform lives, uplift communities, and change the world—one role at a time.

CHAPTER 4:

Trailblazing In Hollywood: Lily Gladstone's Impact On Indigenous Representation

In this chapter, we explore Lily Gladstone's trailblazing journey in Hollywood, her impact on indigenous representation, and her efforts to reshape the entertainment industry from within.

The Hollywood Landscape:

As Lily Gladstone navigates the corridors of Hollywood, she encounters a landscape dominated by traditional power structures, entrenched biases, and systemic barriers to entry. Despite the industry's reputation for exclusivity and homogeneity, Gladstone remains undeterred, determined to carve out a space for herself and fellow indigenous artists.

Pioneering Roles:

Gladstone's ascent in Hollywood begins with her breakthrough performance in "Certain Women," directed by Kelly Reichardt. In this critically acclaimed film, Gladstone defies stereotypes and captivates audiences with her nuanced portrayal of Jamie, a Native American ranch hand grappling with loneliness and longing in rural Montana. Her performance earns widespread praise from critics and peers alike, positioning her as a rising star and a beacon of hope for indigenous representation in mainstream cinema.

Shaping Narratives:

Building on the success of "Certain Women," Gladstone continues to shape narratives and challenge stereotypes through her choice of roles and collaborations. In projects like "First Cow" and "Killers of the Flower Moon," she brings authenticity, depth, and humanity to characters that defy conventional expectations and expand the boundaries of indigenous storytelling. Through her work, she strives to amplify indigenous voices, reclaim indigenous narratives, and confront the legacy of colonialism and cultural erasure in mainstream media.

Advocacy and Activism:

Beyond her work on screen, Gladstone is a vocal advocate for indigenous rights, representation, and cultural sovereignty in Hollywood and beyond. She uses her platform to raise awareness about the unique challenges facing indigenous artists and communities, from cultural appropriation and misrepresentation to lack of access and opportunity. Through speaking engagements, interviews, and social media activism, she amplifies indigenous voices, advocates for systemic change, and fosters greater inclusivity and equity in the entertainment industry.

Empowering the Next Generation:

As a trailblazer in Hollywood, Gladstone recognizes the importance of mentoring and supporting the next generation of indigenous talent. Through mentorship programs, workshops, and outreach initiatives, she provides guidance, encouragement, and practical advice to aspiring indigenous actors, filmmakers, and storytellers. By sharing her experiences, insights, and lessons learned, she empowers emerging artists to navigate the complexities of the industry, overcome obstacles, and pursue their creative aspirations with confidence and resilience.

Cultural Preservation and Revitalization:

In addition to her work in mainstream cinema, Gladstone remains deeply committed to preserving and revitalizing indigenous languages, cultures, and traditions. Through collaborations with indigenous artists, activists, and organizations, she champions initiatives that celebrate indigenous heritage, promote language revitalization, and honor ancestral knowledge and wisdom. By centering indigenous perspectives and values in her work, she contributes to a broader cultural renaissance that affirms indigenous identity, resilience, and sovereignty in the face of ongoing colonization and assimilation.

Legacy and Impact:

As Lily Gladstone's influence continues to grow, her legacy as a trailblazer and cultural icon in Hollywood is secure. Through her pioneering roles, advocacy efforts, and commitment to cultural preservation, she has reshaped the landscape of indigenous representation in mainstream media, paving the way for greater visibility, authenticity, and diversity in storytelling. Her impact extends far beyond the silver screen, inspiring indigenous artists and audiences around the world to reclaim their voices, reclaim their stories, and reclaim their power in an industry that too often overlooks their contributions and experiences.

Through her trailblazing roles, advocacy efforts, and commitment to empowering indigenous communities, she has transformed the entertainment industry from within, challenging stereotypes, amplifying voices, and reshaping narratives to reflect the rich diversity of human experience. As she continues to trailblaze, advocate, and inspire, she leaves an indelible mark on the cultural landscape of Hollywood and the world, reminding us all of the transformative power of storytelling to heal, educate, and unite across boundaries of culture, language, and tradition.

CHAPTER 5

Cultural Resilience: Lily Gladstone's Impact On Indigenous Communities

In this chapter, we explore Lily Gladstone's profound impact on indigenous communities, both within and beyond the entertainment industry. From her advocacy work and philanthropic efforts to her cultural activism and community engagement, Gladstone's commitment to uplifting indigenous voices, perspectives, and experiences has reverberated far and wide, leaving an indelible mark on the cultural landscape of Hollywood and beyond.

Cultural Representation in Media:

At the heart of Gladstone's impact lies her steadfast commitment to advancing indigenous representation in mainstream media. Through her groundbreaking roles in film and television, she has challenged stereotypes, dismantled misconceptions, and humanized indigenous characters in ways that resonate deeply with audiences worldwide. From her portrayal of Mollie Burkhart in "Killers of the Flower Moon" to her nuanced performance in "Certain Women," Gladstone has brought authenticity, depth, and complexity to indigenous storytelling, paving the way for greater visibility and recognition of indigenous talent in

Hollywood.

Empowering Indigenous Voices:

In addition to her on-screen work, Gladstone has been a vocal advocate for empowering indigenous voices behind the scenes. Through her involvement in mentorship programs, talent development initiatives, and advocacy campaigns, she has worked tirelessly to create pathways for aspiring indigenous filmmakers, writers, and producers to break into the industry and tell their own stories. By amplifying indigenous perspectives, experiences, and narratives, Gladstone seeks to foster a more inclusive, equitable, and diverse media landscape that reflects the richness and complexity of indigenous cultures and communities.

Community Engagement and Outreach:

Beyond her work in the entertainment industry, Gladstone has been deeply involved in community engagement and outreach efforts aimed at supporting indigenous communities and promoting cultural resilience. From volunteering with local organizations and charities to participating in cultural events and gatherings, she has used her platform and visibility to raise awareness about indigenous issues, advocate for social justice, and foster solidarity among indigenous peoples worldwide. By connecting with grassroots movements, community leaders, and cultural elders, Gladstone remains rooted in her commitment to serving and uplifting indigenous communities in meaningful and sustainable ways.

Philanthropy and Social Impact:

In addition to her advocacy and outreach work, Gladstone has been a generous philanthropist and supporter of indigenous causes and organizations. Through her financial contributions, fundraising efforts, and strategic partnerships, she has helped to provide critical resources, support services, and opportunities to indigenous communities facing systemic inequities, economic challenges, and cultural marginalization. By leveraging her platform and resources for social impact, Gladstone embodies the spirit of generosity, compassion, and solidarity that defines indigenous values and traditions.

Cultural Activism and Leadership:

As a cultural activist and leader, Gladstone has been at the forefront of efforts to preserve, promote, and revitalize indigenous languages, traditions, and practices. Through her involvement in cultural revitalization projects, language preservation initiatives, and traditional arts programs, she has worked to ensure that indigenous cultures and identities are honored, celebrated, and passed down to future generations. By reclaiming indigenous knowledge, wisdom, and ways of life, Gladstone embodies the resilience, strength, and vibrancy of indigenous cultures in the face of historical trauma, cultural erasure, and systemic oppression.

Impact on Indigenous Youth:

One of Gladstone's most significant contributions has been her impact on indigenous youth, who look up to her as a role model, mentor, and inspiration. Through her advocacy work, public speaking engagements, and educational outreach efforts, she has empowered indigenous youth to embrace their identities, pursue their passions, and strive for excellence in all areas of their lives. By sharing her own journey, struggles, and successes, Gladstone instills in indigenous youth a sense of pride, resilience, and possibility, reminding them of their inherent worth, dignity, and potential to create positive change in their communities and beyond.

Through her work in the entertainment industry, advocacy efforts, community engagement, philanthropy, and cultural activism, she has emerged as a transformative force for positive change, resilience, and empowerment within indigenous communities and beyond. As she continues to trailblaze, inspire, and uplift, Gladstone leaves an indelible legacy of cultural resilience, solidarity, and hope for future generations of indigenous peoples around the world.

CHAPTER 6

The Road Ahead: Lily Gladstone's Vision For The Future Of Indigenous Representation

In this chapter, we delve into Lily Gladstone's vision for the future of indigenous representation in Hollywood and beyond. As she reflects on her journey, challenges, and triumphs, Gladstone offers insights, aspirations, and strategies for advancing the cause of indigenous visibility, authenticity, and empowerment in the entertainment industry.

Reflecting on the Journey:

As Lily Gladstone looks back on her career thus far, she acknowledges the progress made in indigenous representation while recognizing the ongoing challenges and obstacles that persist. From her humble beginnings on the Blackfeet Reservation to her breakout roles in Hollywood, Gladstone reflects on the pivotal moments, transformative experiences, and formative influences that have shaped her identity as an artist, activist, and advocate for indigenous rights and representation.

Celebrating Successes:

Despite the barriers and biases, she has encountered along the way, Gladstone takes pride in the strides made by indigenous artists and storytellers in recent years. From groundbreaking films like "Smoke Signals" and "Dances with Wolves" to critically acclaimed series like "Reservation Dogs" and "Rutherford Falls," indigenous voices are increasingly being heard, recognized, and celebrated on screen. Gladstone highlights the achievements of her peers, mentors, and collaborators in reshaping the cultural landscape of Hollywood and amplifying indigenous stories, perspectives, and experiences for global audiences.

Championing Diversity and Inclusion:

As Gladstone envisions the future of indigenous representation, she emphasizes the importance of diversity, inclusion, and equity in all aspects of the entertainment industry. From casting decisions and creative leadership to storytelling approaches and marketing strategies, she calls for greater representation of indigenous talent, narratives, and cultures across genres, formats, and platforms. By championing diverse voices, perspectives, and experiences, Gladstone believes that Hollywood can foster greater empathy, understanding, and connection among audiences worldwide.

Empowering Indigenous Filmmakers:

In addition to advocating for greater visibility and inclusion, Gladstone is committed to empowering indigenous filmmakers to tell their own stories on their own terms. Through mentorship programs, funding initiatives, and collaborative partnerships, she seeks to provide aspiring indigenous directors, writers, and producers with the resources, support, and opportunities they need to bring their visions to life. By centering indigenous perspectives and voices behind the camera, she believes that Hollywood can catalyze a transformative shift in storytelling that reflects the richness, complexity, and diversity of indigenous cultures and communities.

Addressing Systemic Inequities:

Despite the progress made in recent years, Gladstone acknowledges that systemic inequities and injustices continue to plague the entertainment industry, particularly for indigenous artists and storytellers. From unequal access to funding and distribution to pervasive stereotypes and misrepresentations, she confronts the structural barriers and biases that perpetuate marginalization and exclusion in Hollywood. By advocating for systemic change, Gladstone aims to dismantle the entrenched power dynamics and colonial legacies that undermine indigenous sovereignty, dignity, and self-determination in the media landscape.

Cultivating Cultural Sovereignty:

At the heart of Gladstone's vision for the future lies the
concept of cultural sovereignty – the inherent right of
indigenous peoples to control and shape their own
narratives, images, and destinies in the media. By reclaiming
indigenous languages, traditions, and storytelling practices,
she seeks to decolonize the cultural landscape of Hollywood
and foster a more inclusive, equitable, and respectful
environment for indigenous artists and communities.
Through collaborations with indigenous-led initiatives,
organizations, and institutions, she works to cultivate spaces
of cultural sovereignty where indigenous voices are honored,
valued, and celebrated as vital contributors to the tapestry of
human creativity and expression.

Inspiring the Next Generation:

As Gladstone looks ahead to the future, she is mindful of the
impact she can have on the next generation of indigenous
artists, activists, and leaders. Through her advocacy work,
mentorship initiatives, and educational outreach efforts, she
seeks to inspire and empower young indigenous people to
pursue their passions, amplify their voices, and create
positive change in their communities and beyond. By sharing
her own journey, struggles, and successes, she hopes to

instill in future generations a sense of pride, resilience, and possibility as they navigate the complexities of identity, representation, and belonging in an ever-changing world.

Lily Gladstone's vision for the future of indigenous representation is one of hope, resilience, and empowerment. By championing diversity, inclusion, and cultural sovereignty in Hollywood and beyond, she seeks to reshape the narrative landscape of mainstream media and create a more equitable, inclusive, and authentic environment for indigenous artists and storytellers. As she continues to trailblaze, advocate, and inspire, Gladstone leaves an indelible mark on the cultural fabric of Hollywood and the world, reminding us all of the transformative power of storytelling to heal, educate, and unite across boundaries of culture, language, and tradition.

CHAPTER 7

Legacy And Future Endeavors: Lily Gladstone's Impact On The Entertainment Industry

In this chapter, we delve into Lily Gladstone's enduring legacy in the entertainment industry and explore her future endeavors as she continues to push boundaries, challenge norms, and redefine what it means to be an indigenous actor and cultural advocate in Hollywood and beyond.

The Evolution of Indigenous Representation:

Gladstone's journey in the entertainment industry has coincided with a broader shift in attitudes towards indigenous representation in mainstream media. Over the years, indigenous actors, filmmakers, and storytellers have increasingly demanded authentic, nuanced portrayals of indigenous characters and narratives, challenging stereotypes, biases, and misconceptions that have long plagued indigenous representation in Hollywood. Gladstone's groundbreaking roles in films like "Certain Women" and "Killers of the Flower Moon" have played a pivotal role in this evolution, showcasing the depth, complexity, and humanity of indigenous experiences in ways that resonate with audiences worldwide.

Trailblazing in Hollywood:

As one of the few indigenous actors to achieve widespread recognition and acclaim in Hollywood, Gladstone has paved the way for future generations of indigenous talent to break into the industry and thrive on their own terms. Through her perseverance, talent, and commitment to authenticity, she has shattered barriers, opened doors, and challenged industry norms, demonstrating that indigenous actors have the talent, skill, and versatility to excel in diverse roles across film, television, and theater. By carving out a space for herself in Hollywood, Gladstone has inspired countless indigenous actors to pursue their dreams and make their voices heard in an industry that has often overlooked or marginalized their contributions.

Advocacy and Representation:

Beyond her work on screen, Gladstone has been a vocal advocate for greater representation and inclusion of indigenous voices in all aspects of the entertainment industry. From advocating for more indigenous writers, directors, and producers to championing indigenous-led storytelling and production companies, she has worked tirelessly to create more opportunities and platforms for indigenous creatives to tell their own stories on their own terms. By leveraging her platform and visibility, Gladstone continues to push for systemic change within the industry, challenging power structures, biases, and inequities that have historically excluded indigenous voices from mainstream media.

Impact on Indigenous Communities:

Gladstone's impact extends far beyond the confines of Hollywood, reaching indigenous communities worldwide. Through her advocacy work, philanthropic efforts, and community engagement initiatives, she has uplifted indigenous voices, perspectives, and experiences, fostering a sense of pride, resilience, and empowerment among indigenous peoples everywhere. By using her platform to raise awareness about indigenous issues, advocate for social justice, and amplify indigenous voices, Gladstone has become a beacon of hope and inspiration for indigenous communities facing systemic inequities, cultural erasure, and historical trauma.

Future Endeavors:

As Gladstone looks towards the future, her commitment to advancing indigenous representation and cultural advocacy remains unwavering. With several projects in the pipeline, including film roles, television appearances, and advocacy campaigns, she continues to push boundaries, challenge norms, and amplify indigenous voices in the entertainment industry and beyond. Whether she's working on a new film project, mentoring aspiring indigenous actors, or speaking out on behalf of indigenous communities, Gladstone's passion, determination, and resilience continue to drive her forward as she seeks to make a lasting impact on the world around her.

Lily Gladstone's legacy in the entertainment industry is one of trailblazing courage, unwavering determination, and profound impact. From her groundbreaking roles on screen to her advocacy work off screen, she has left an indelible mark on Hollywood and beyond, inspiring generations of indigenous talent to pursue their dreams and make their voices heard in an industry that has often overlooked or marginalized their contributions. As she continues to chart her own path and blaze new trails, Gladstone remains a beacon of hope, resilience, and empowerment for indigenous communities around the world, reminding us all of the power of storytelling to change hearts, minds, and lives.

CHAPTER 8

Reflections and Inspirations: Lily Gladstone's Journey

In this chapter, we delve into Lily Gladstone's journey, reflecting on the experiences, challenges, and inspirations that have shaped her into the remarkable actor, advocate, and cultural ambassador she is today. From her upbringing on the Blackfeet Reservation to her breakthrough roles in Hollywood, we explore the pivotal moments and profound influences that have guided Gladstone on her path to success.

Childhood on the Blackfeet Reservation:

Gladstone's journey begins in the rugged landscapes of the Blackfeet Reservation in northwestern Montana, where she was born and raised. Growing up surrounded by the natural beauty and cultural richness of her indigenous heritage, Gladstone developed a deep connection to her roots, finding solace, inspiration, and belonging in the traditions, stories, and values passed down through generations of her family. From an early age, she was immersed in the vibrant tapestry of Blackfeet culture, learning the language, customs, and ceremonies that would shape her identity and worldview for years to come.

Early Influences and Inspirations:

As a child, Gladstone was captivated by the power of storytelling, finding refuge in the pages of books, the flickering images of films, and the vibrant performances of local storytellers and elders. These early influences sparked her imagination, fueling her passion for acting and performance as a means of connecting with others, sharing stories, and exploring the complexities of human experience. Inspired by the resilience, creativity, and cultural pride of her indigenous community, Gladstone began to dream of a future in which she could use her talents to make a difference in the world.

Navigating Identity and Belonging:

Like many indigenous youths, Gladstone grappled with questions of identity, belonging, and cultural heritage as she navigated the complexities of adolescence and young adulthood. Moving away from the reservation at the age of 11, she found herself straddling two worlds – the familiar landscapes of her indigenous heritage and the unfamiliar terrain of suburban America. Wrestling with feelings of displacement, alienation, and cultural disconnection, Gladstone embarked on a journey of self-discovery, seeking to reconcile the diverse strands of her identity and forge a sense of belonging that honored both her indigenous roots and her aspirations for the future.

Educational Pursuits and Artistic Exploration:

Despite the challenges of adjusting to life outside the reservation, Gladstone remained steadfast in her pursuit of education and artistic expression. Attending Mountlake Terrace High School in Washington state, she excelled academically and artistically, finding opportunities to explore her passion for acting, storytelling, and cultural advocacy. Whether performing in school plays, participating in community theater productions, or immersing herself in the study of literature, history, and indigenous culture, Gladstone honed her craft and cultivated the skills, resilience, and determination that would propel her toward a career in the arts.

Navigating the Entertainment Industry:

After graduating from high school, Gladstone embarked on a journey into the heart of the entertainment industry, determined to carve out a space for herself in an industry that often overlooked or marginalized indigenous talent. Armed with talent, tenacity, and a fierce determination to succeed, she navigated the challenges of auditions, rejections, and setbacks with grace and resilience, refusing to compromise her integrity or authenticity for the sake of fame or fortune. Drawing inspiration from her indigenous heritage, Gladstone forged ahead, blazing trails, challenging stereotypes, and redefining what it means to be a Native American actor in Hollywood.

Breakthrough Roles and Career Milestones:

Gladstone's perseverance and talent soon caught the attention of filmmakers, casting directors, and industry insiders, leading to a series of breakthrough roles and career milestones that would catapult her into the spotlight. From her unforgettable performance in Kelly Reichardt's "Certain Women" to her acclaimed portrayal of Mollie Burkhart in Martin Scorsese's "Killers of the Flower Moon," Gladstone captivated audiences and critics alike with her authenticity, vulnerability, and emotional depth. With each new role, she pushed boundaries, challenged norms, and expanded the possibilities for indigenous representation in mainstream media, earning accolades, awards, and widespread acclaim for her groundbreaking work.

Cultural Advocacy and Community Engagement:

Throughout her career, Gladstone has remained deeply committed to cultural advocacy, community engagement, and social justice, using her platform and visibility to uplift indigenous voices, perspectives, and experiences in the entertainment industry and beyond. Whether speaking out on issues of representation, advocating for greater inclusion and diversity in Hollywood, or supporting grassroots organizations and initiatives in indigenous communities, she has been a tireless champion for change, equality, and empowerment. Through her advocacy work, philanthropic efforts, and community partnerships, Gladstone continues to inspire and empower indigenous youth, artists, and activists to reclaim their narratives, celebrate their heritage, and create a more just and equitable world for future generations.

Lily Gladstone's journey is a testament to the power of resilience, determination, and cultural pride in overcoming adversity, embracing diversity, and forging a path of purpose and passion in pursuit of one's dreams. From her humble beginnings on the Blackfeet Reservation to her trailblazing career in Hollywood, she has remained true to herself, her heritage, and her values, inspiring countless others to do the same. As she continues to chart her own course and make her mark on the world, Gladstone's journey serves as a beacon of hope, resilience, and inspiration for indigenous communities and aspiring artists everywhere, reminding us all of the transformative power of storytelling to change lives, challenge perceptions, and build bridges across cultures and communities.

CHAPTER 9

Personal Growth and Development

In the intricate tapestry of Lily Gladstone's life, personal growth and development form the vibrant threads that weave through her journey. This chapter delves into the transformative moments, the lessons learned, and the evolving perspectives that have shaped her as both an individual and an artist.

From the vast expanse of the Blackfeet Reservation where she spent her formative years to the bustling cities where her career flourished, Gladstone's path has been a mosaic of experiences that have contributed to her growth.

Embracing Identity and Heritage

Rooted in her indigenous heritage, Gladstone's journey of personal growth is intertwined with a deep exploration of identity. Growing up on the Blackfeet Reservation provided her with a strong sense of community and connection to her cultural roots. As she navigated the complexities of adolescence and young adulthood, she grappled with questions of identity and belonging, forging a deeper understanding of her place in the world.

Artistic Exploration and Self-Discovery

For Gladstone, acting became not only a creative outlet but also a means of self-expression and exploration. Immersing herself in the world of theater, she discovered the power of storytelling as a tool for personal and collective healing. Each role she inhabited became a canvas on which she could paint the nuances of human experience, delving into the depths of emotion and empathy.

Navigating Success and Challenges

As her career gained momentum, Gladstone faced the dual challenges of success and scrutiny. The spotlight brought both opportunities and pressures, forcing her to confront insecurities and navigate the complexities of fame. Yet, amidst the whirlwind of public attention, she remained grounded in her values and principles, finding strength in authenticity and resilience.

Cultivating Resilience and Adaptability

Throughout her journey, Gladstone has embodied a spirit of resilience and adaptability, embracing the inevitable twists and turns of life with grace and courage. Whether facing professional setbacks or personal challenges, she has approached each obstacle as an opportunity for growth, drawing strength from her inner resilience and unwavering determination.

Finding Balance and Harmony

In the midst of her hectic schedule and demanding career, Gladstone has prioritized self-care and holistic well-being. From mindfulness practices to time spent in nature, she has cultivated rituals that nourish her mind, body, and spirit, finding balance amidst the chaos of modern life.

Looking Towards the Future

As Gladstone continues to evolve and grow, she remains committed to her journey of personal and artistic exploration. With each new role and project, she embraces the opportunity to delve deeper into the complexities of the human experience, using her platform to amplify marginalized voices and spark meaningful conversations.

Lily Gladstone's journey of personal growth and development is a testament to the transformative power of self-discovery and resilience. From her roots on the Blackfeet Reservation to the global stage of Hollywood, she navigated the complexities of life with courage, grace, and authenticity. As she continues to chart her course, she serves as an inspiration to all who dare to embark on the journey of self-discovery.

CHAPTER 10

Legacy and Impact

In the final chapter of Lily Gladstone's biography, we explore the enduring legacy and profound impact of her life and work. From her groundbreaking achievements in film to her advocacy for Indigenous representation, Gladstone's influence extends far beyond the silver screen, leaving an indelible mark on both the entertainment industry and society as a whole.

Pioneering Representation

Throughout her career, Gladstone has been a trailblazer for Indigenous representation in Hollywood. By fearlessly taking on roles that authentically reflect her heritage and experiences, she has shattered stereotypes and paved the way for future generations of Indigenous actors and storytellers. Her presence on screen serves as a beacon of hope and inspiration for marginalized communities, proving that diversity and inclusion are not only necessary but also transformative forces within the industry.

Amplifying Marginalized Voices

Beyond her performances, Gladstone has used her platform to amplify the voices of marginalized communities, advocating for greater representation and inclusion in all aspects of the entertainment industry. Through her advocacy work and philanthropic efforts, she has championed causes ranging from Indigenous rights to LGBTQ+ equality, leveraging her influence to spark meaningful change and foster a more inclusive society.

Empowering the Next Generation

As a role model and mentor, Gladstone is committed to empowering the next generation of artists and activists, providing guidance, support, and encouragement to aspiring talent from underrepresented backgrounds. Through workshops, speaking engagements, and community outreach initiatives, she shares her wisdom and experiences, inspiring others to pursue their passions and make their voices heard.

Redefining Success and Impact

For Gladstone, success is not measured solely by accolades or box office receipts but by the impact she has on the world around her. Whether through her performances on screen or her advocacy work off-screen, she strives to make a meaningful difference in the lives of others, using her talents and platform for the greater good. Her legacy is not defined by fame or fortune but by the hearts she touches and the lives she changes for the better.

Honoring Heritage and Tradition

At the heart of Gladstone's legacy is a deep reverence for her Indigenous heritage and traditions. Throughout her journey, she has remained grounded in the teachings of her ancestors, drawing strength from their wisdom and resilience. By honoring her cultural heritage and preserving traditional practices, she ensures that the legacy of her people lives on for future generations to cherish and celebrate.

Looking Towards the Future

As Gladstone reflects on her journey and the legacy she leaves behind, she remains optimistic about the future of Indigenous representation in the entertainment industry and beyond. With each passing year, progress is made, barriers are broken, and voices once silenced are heard. She looks forward to a future where diversity and inclusion are not only embraced but celebrated, where stories from all walks of life are given the platform they deserve.

CHAPTER 11

Reflections and Gratitude

In this final chapter of Lily Gladstone's biography, we delve into her reflections on her journey, the challenges she has faced, and the gratitude she holds for the experiences that have shaped her life and career. From humble beginnings to Hollywood acclaim, Gladstone's story is one of perseverance, passion, and profound gratitude for the opportunities she has been given.

Embracing the Journey

As Gladstone looks back on her career, she is filled with a sense of gratitude for the winding path that has led her to where she is today. From her early days on the Blackfeet Reservation to the bright lights of Hollywood, every step of her journey has been a lesson in resilience and determination. She cherishes the highs and lows, the triumphs and setbacks, knowing that each experience has contributed to her growth and evolution as an artist and a human being.

Finding Purpose in Adversity

Throughout her life, Gladstone has encountered her fair share of obstacles and challenges. From navigating the complexities of Hollywood to confronting systemic barriers to Indigenous representation, she has faced adversity with grace and resilience. Rather than allowing setbacks to derail her, she has used them as fuel to propel her forward, finding purpose in the struggle and strength in the journey.

Gratitude for Support and Community

At every step of her journey, Gladstone has been buoyed by the unwavering support of her family, friends, and community. From her parents' unwavering belief in her dreams to the encouragement of her mentors and peers, she is deeply grateful for the love and support that has sustained her through the highs and lows of her career. She also acknowledges the broader community of fans and supporters who have championed her work and celebrated her successes, recognizing that she does not walk this path alone.

Acknowledging Privilege and Responsibility

As her star continues to rise, Gladstone is mindful of the privilege and responsibility that come with success. She recognizes the importance of using her platform to uplift others, amplify marginalized voices, and effect positive change in the world. With privilege comes responsibility, and she is committed to using her voice and influence for the greater good, advocating for justice, equality, and inclusion for all.

Finding Joy in the Journey

Despite the challenges and complexities of life in the spotlight, Gladstone remains grounded in gratitude and joy. She finds solace in the simple pleasures of life – the beauty of nature, the warmth of human connection, and the joy of storytelling. She cherishes each moment as a precious gift, embracing the fullness of life with an open heart and a grateful spirit.

Paying It Forward

As Gladstone reflects on her journey, she is inspired to pay it forward, offering support and encouragement to the next generation of artists and activists. She knows firsthand the power of mentorship and believes in the importance of lifting others as we climb. Through mentorship programs, scholarships, and community outreach initiatives, she seeks to empower others to pursue their passions and realize their dreams, just as she has been empowered by those ahead.

CHAPTER 12

Legacy and Continuing Impact

In this final chapter of Lily Gladstone's biography, we explore the legacy she leaves behind and the continuing impact of her work on the entertainment industry and beyond. From her groundbreaking performances to her advocacy for Indigenous representation, Gladstone's influence extends far beyond the screen, leaving an indelible mark on the world of film and inspiring future generations of artists and activists.

The Power of Representation

One of the most significant aspects of Gladstone's legacy is her role in advancing Indigenous representation in Hollywood. Throughout her career, she has been a vocal advocate for greater diversity and inclusion in the entertainment industry, challenging stereotypes and amplifying marginalized voices. By bringing authentic Indigenous stories to the screen and portraying complex, multifaceted characters, Gladstone has helped to shift the narrative surrounding Indigenous peoples and cultures, paving the way for greater visibility and representation in mainstream media.

Lily Gladstone

Inspiring Future Generations

Gladstone's impact extends beyond her on-screen performances to her role as a mentor and role model for aspiring artists, particularly within Indigenous communities. Through her advocacy work, outreach efforts, and engagement with fans, she has inspired countless individuals to pursue their passions and embrace their cultural heritage with pride. By sharing her own journey and experiences, she has provided a roadmap for others to follow, proving that with determination, perseverance, and a strong sense of identity, anything is possible.

Elevating Indigenous Voices

As a proud member of the Blackfeet Nation, Gladstone has been a tireless champion for Indigenous rights and sovereignty, using her platform to elevate Indigenous voices and advocate for social and political change. Whether speaking out against environmental injustice, advocating for Indigenous land rights, or supporting Indigenous-led initiatives, she has been a vocal ally and ally for Indigenous communities around the world. Her commitment to justice, equality, and reconciliation serves as a beacon of hope for Indigenous peoples everywhere, inspiring them to stand up, speak out, and fight for a better future.

Leaving a Lasting Impact

As Gladstone's career continues to evolve, her impact on the entertainment industry and beyond will only continue to grow. Through her groundbreaking performances, advocacy work, and commitment to social justice, she has left an indelible mark on the world, inspiring others to follow in her footsteps and make a difference in their own communities. Whether through her work on screen, her activism behind the scenes, or her engagement with fans and followers, she has touched the lives of countless individuals and left behind a legacy that will endure for generations to come.

Lily's legacy is one of trailblazing courage, visionary leadership, and unwavering commitment to justice and equality. Through her artistry, advocacy, and activism, she has shattered stereotypes, challenged conventions, and paved the way for a more inclusive and equitable future. As we reflect on her remarkable journey and the impact she has had on the world, we are reminded of the power of storytelling to inspire change, foster empathy, and unite communities in the pursuit of a common goal. Lily Gladstone may have reached the end of her own journey, but her legacy will continue to shine brightly, illuminating the path for future generations to follow.

CONCLUSION

As we conclude the remarkable journey through Lily Gladstone's life, it's impossible not to be profoundly moved by the depth of her experiences, the resilience she has demonstrated, and the impact she continues to make in the world of film and beyond. From her roots on the Blackfeet Reservation in Montana to the global stage of Hollywood, Lily's story is a testament to the power of perseverance, passion, and the pursuit of one's dreams.

Throughout this biography, we have delved into the formative years of Lily's upbringing, where the landscapes of the reservation shaped her identity and instilled in her a deep connection to her Native American heritage. We've learned of her family's unwavering support, the values they imparted, and the sacrifices they made to nurture Lily's talents and aspirations. From her parents' home, which served as a refuge and a source of strength, to the vast expanses of Montana that fueled her imagination and sense of belonging, Lily's journey began with a profound appreciation for her roots.

As she ventured beyond the reservation and into the world of acting, Lily faced both the triumphs and tribulations that come with pursuing a career in the arts. We've witnessed her navigate the challenges of stereotyped casting, the frustrations of rejection, and the moments of doubt that tested her resolve. Yet, through it all, Lily remained steadfast in her commitment to her craft, drawing inspiration from her community, her culture, and the stories that demanded to be told.

The turning point in Lily's career came with her breakout role in Kelly Reichardt's "Certain Women," a film that showcased her immense talent and marked her arrival on the international stage. With minimal dialogue but a profound presence, Lily captivated audiences and critics alike, earning accolades for her raw, authentic portrayal of Jamie, a Native American rancher navigating the complexities of love and longing. It was a performance that resonated deeply with viewers, transcending cultural boundaries and cementing Lily's reputation as a rising star in the industry.

From "Certain Women" to her groundbreaking role in Martin Scorsese's "Killers of the Flower Moon," Lily continued to defy expectations and challenge conventions, blazing a trail for indigenous performers and storytellers. Her Golden Globe nomination for Best Actress in a Drama Motion Picture was not just a personal triumph but a historic moment for representation and inclusion in Hollywood, underscoring the importance of diverse voices and narratives on screen.

But beyond the glitz and glamour of the red carpet, Lily remains grounded in her commitment to using her platform for social change and advocacy. We've seen her champion causes close to her heart, from supporting indigenous artists and filmmakers to raising awareness about issues facing Native American communities. Through her work on and off-screen, Lily has become a beacon of hope and inspiration for aspiring actors, marginalized voices, and anyone who dares to dream big.

As we bid farewell to Lily Gladstone's story, it's clear that her journey is far from over. With her talent, passion, and unwavering determination, Lily continues to push boundaries, break barriers, and leave an indelible mark on the world around her. Whether she's gracing the silver screen, treading the boards of a theater stage, or lending her voice to important causes, Lily's legacy will endure as a testament to the power of storytelling, the resilience of the human spirit, and the enduring quest for authenticity and representation in all its forms.

In the end, Lily Gladstone's biography is not just a chronicle of one woman's extraordinary life but a celebration of the boundless possibilities that await those who dare to dream, persevere, and believe in the power of their own voices. As we close this chapter, let us carry forward the lessons learned from Lily's journey – to embrace our roots, chase our passions, and always strive for authenticity, empathy, and understanding in everything we do. For in the end, it is our stories that connect us, inspire us, and remind us of the beauty and resilience of the human spirit. Lily Gladstone's story is one that will continue to inspire generations to come, a shining example of what it means to live boldly, love fiercely, and leave a lasting legacy of hope and possibility in our wake.

Made in the USA
Thornton, CO
12/01/24 12:28:43

66dc693d-53eb-4cf9-97bd-0b7fd3714b7bR01